Interior Design:

An Essential Guide On Home Decorating With Luxurious Style.

Austin Knight

Table of Contents

Introduction

Congratulations on downloading *Interior Design: An Essential Guide On Home Decorating With Luxurious Style.*

When your enthusiasm for your current interior motif fades, it can be easy to slip in to an ambivalent rut, but by purchasing this book you have made a decision to go in the other direction and fight back against ambivalence with a current and trendy update to your home's style instead. It doesn't matter if you already have a clear idea of what you want to do next or if you are still looking for the right inspiration, the following pages will do wonders to set you on the right path.

It doesn't matter what your current plans are it is always nice to have a second opinion, unfortunately, with so much home improvement advice available at practically every turn, it can be difficult to separate the wheat from the chaff which is why the following chapters will discuss everything you need to know about the new Victorian style, the midcentury modern style and the beach stone style. First, however, you will learn the basic principles of interior design which you will want to consider when you are planning out your own plan of attack moving forward. You will then learn about the core principles of the three styles that are going to be discussed in detail before learning how to update your living room, kitchen, bedrooms and bathrooms in each style in a way that is so flawless that visitors to your home won't believe you didn't have to pay someone to do it for you.

There are plenty of books on this subject in the market, thanks again for choosing this one! Every effort was made to ensure it is better and full of as much useful information as possible, please enjoy!

Chapter 1: Understanding Interior Design

While some individuals are constantly updating their homes with the latest styles and most up-to-date reflections of their inner selves, most people don't update their living space more than once per decade, if that. It is easy how someone could come to be unhappy with the current look of their personal space, as redecorating can often be thought of as a chore or something that can only be done with a major overhaul to the existing space.

This doesn't have to be the case, however, and it is important to approach the experience with the idea that it can be a fun way to help your home reflect who you are as a person right here, right now. Do you already have some great ideas for your existing space? Consider the following interior design fundamentals to ensure that you are on the right track.

Consider the visual weight of the room: Visual weight is a good way to determine the flow and potential arrangement you want to use in a room. Overall there are three different ways to think about visual weight, the first of which is often labeled as asymmetrical. Asymmetrical layouts are often considered the most visually stimulating of the visual weight layouts and are notable for their intentional imbalance when it comes to décor and furniture in a few key areas. While this can cause the room to feel more chaotic, it can also make it seem more casual, while also making it seem more interesting at the same time.

On the other hand, symmetrical room designs are quite common, simply because most people are naturally drawn to symmetrical patterns. While this style is often considered pleasing to the eye, it can be difficult to maintain the symmetry for the long term in spaces that are used on the regular. Unless you are committed to keeping the symmetry up in the long term it might be better to go with an asymmetrical solution instead. Finally, a radial style puts a central element at the nexus of a space and lets everything else flow around it. For example, you would have an extremely nice table and mantle piece in the middle of your lounge room, then you would design the room around the colors and material of these items. This style is difficult to pull off correctly unless the space in question was designed for it specifically as it will come off feeling forced in most cases otherwise.

   Consider the scale and proportion: When it comes to updating your look, you are going to want to take a step back and evaluate the space as analytically as possible. Understanding the scale of the room as well as its size is key to determining how to fill it successfully. When it comes to considering proportion, keep the following in mind for the best results, first and foremost, it is important to keep in mind the central color that will ultimately define the space. Repeating that color at key points throughout the room will not only give the room a renewed sense of purpose, it will naturally proportion out the space properly.

   Additionally, you will want to keep the amount of light that the space receives in mind as both light and shadow serve to enhance or minimize the apparent space a room has on offer. As with color you will also want to consider repeating patterns, shapes or textures in a single room, or even over multiple rooms to give the illusion of maximum space. The space that is available is equally important and you will want to make a point of arranged objects in a room with an eye to the proportion it generates.

   Decide on the focal point: When it comes to deciding what you want to do with a given room moving forward, the first thing you are going to want to do is to choose the focal point that you are going to design the new room around. A room that is larger can have multiple focal points, but every room needs at least one place that is naturally going to draw the eye of those who enter. The goal of a good focal point is to leave a lasting impression while also being an obvious part of a larger whole. Common examples in this vain include things like a large television or fireplace, but a focal point can be anything eye catching including things like artwork, furniture, even a wall that is painted differently than the surrounding walls. Remember, a good focal point draws the eye first without completely hogging all the attention.

Don't forget the rhythm: When it comes to music, rhythm can be thought of as the pulse, the beat of what's happening; when it comes to interior design it can be thought of as organized continuity or a deliberate recurrence of movement. It is important that your space has movement, a natural flow that leads the eye around the room. This can be accomplished in several different ways, one of which is known as repetition whereby you repeat a specific element at several points throughout the room so that the eye is naturally drawn from one to the next. A variation of this is known as progression where you take a basic element and they alter one or more of its qualities throughout the space. Alternatively, you can put contrasting elements in opposed places in the room to achieve the same results with the opposite effect.

Balance rhythm with harmony: While rhythm is useful when it comes to creating a feeling of excitement in a room, harmony is used to create a sense of peace or restfulness in a room. Harmony is created when all the elements of the room act together to send a specific message. Some rooms will need a balance of harmony as well as rhythm while others will simply need one or the other. Primary living spaces often have more rhythm than harmony, as do kitchens which reflect the more active nature of the use of these rooms. Bedrooms are often more harmonious than rhythmic to promote a restful night's sleep.

Consider the unity: Along with harmony and continuity is required if you hope to link multiple interior spaces together to give not just a room but your home an overall flow. This means that you are going to want to avoid using multiple different styles in the home and instead choose one that is going to work across multiple rooms. While this can be a more dramatic undertaking than simply whipping a given room into shape, the results will create a much more natural flow that is not interrupted by countless different and conflicting styles as visitors move from room to room. This doesn't mean every room has to look exactly the same, it just means that certain elements need to be present in each to give the space a unified feel.

Let the space reflect who you are: It is important to include some personality in each room that really makes the space your own. This can be done through the proper use of accessories that reflect your personal style. While you typically want things like area rugs, pillows, tchotchkes and the like to support the overall theme, this is where you are going to find the most leeway when it comes to mixing things up somewhat. Just be sure not to go overboard, a little accessorizing goes a long way. But keep in mind too much accessorizing will hinder and clutter the room/area.

If you feel as though the space that you have created appears too sterile, then this might be caused by following a given outline to closely. A good way to counteract this is by adding in a bit of whimsy to the proceedings. Something silly or unexpected can go a long way towards making a room feel more inviting, it doesn't have to be much, a dash of the unexpected is all that most rooms need.

Don't neglect the details: When it comes to putting together a room that not only looks nice, but looks as though it was created by a professional, it is important to think about everything down to the smallest detail. Little things like the trim of a lamp shade or the cover on the light switch might seem like nitpicking, but the truth of the matter is that they as important to the overall effect that the room portrays as the major elements. Attention to the little details is what separates a room that looks nice from one that looks designed with a purpose.

Whilst you are selecting items to purchase for your room don't buy the cheapest items in the store, you need to buy slight more expensive items if you are going to showcase your room in a luxurious style. This is also achievable on a budget as you can look online for secondhand items in near perfect condition.

Chapter 2: Choosing a Style That is Right for You

When it comes to choosing a new direction to take your home in, the first step to doing so properly is going to be choosing the style that best suits the property as well as meshes most with your personality. The styles that are currently in vogue are new Victorian, midcentury modern and beach stone and each are described in detail below. Here is a helpful word of advice, when designing you're home it is immensely helpful to have a workbook and a folder, in order to plan out each room and store your ideas from different magazines and shops.

New Victorian: Traditional Victorian design drew its inspiration for the Industrial Revolution, which allowed the middle class to increase their wealth, and in turn their homes, substantially. This meant lots of fabric and wood, the bigger and heavier the better, haha. When it comes to fabrics there was lots of velvet, damask and chintzes and practically everything was ablaze with patterns which would typically contain everything from damasks and flora or fauna to things like stripes and geometric patterns. Colors from the time tended to lean towards the subdued and warm end of the pallet.

The new Victorian style came about both as those who owned traditional Victorian property sought to update their homes, and those with other types of properties strove to add a touch of the Victorian home class to their own homes. This style can accurately be described as a mix of old and new, typically an older style of major focal pieces, typically with some new modern accents thrown in. The biggest key to pulling of this style is restraint, you will want to move carefully as you mesh the two styles as things can quickly turn messy if you aren't careful. The goal is to create something that feels out of time, not like it was furnished from thrift store finds and chain stores. Good examples of this style include things like:

- Pairing a Victorian table with steel chairs
- Reupholster a modern low profile couch with a classic damask fabric
- Reupholster an old dining room set with a bold modern print
- Paint damaged antiques using modern sensibilities

Homes in the Victorian area were the epitome of status symbols which meant filling them with as many high-quality things as possible. This means that the best way to add a bit of a Victorian flair to any room is with lots of heavy wooden pieces including frames and lamps as well as furniture. Additionally, any modern pieces that you add into the space are going to need to be of an equal quality to ensure the effect is maintained. Another good choice is adding in a fireplace mantle or even an entire electric fireplace that is designed to evoke the time period in question. Salvaged pieces from old Victorian homes are also a great choice as they can add a dash of authenticity to the proceedings as well.

While the heading of heavy old accent pieces gives you lots of options when it comes to personalizing the style so that it is right for you, the major takeaway with this style is that you are typically going to need more space for this type of style unless you don't mind walking around large vanity pieces on the regular.

Midcentury modern: Midcentury modern can be a difficult classification to nail down specifically, simply because it is often misattributed to so many different, and often conflicting, styles. Broadly, this term can be applied to graphic design, furniture and architecture that ages its design from the period dating from around 1935 to around 1965. This timeframe saw a sharp increase in influence from the modernist movement that began at the end of the 1800s and really took hold starting in the period post-World War I.

When it comes to colors for this type of interior design choice, colors tend to skew towards neutral tones in darker shades along with accent colors that are more saturated. The furniture that is related to this design aesthetic is easily definable thanks to its combination of smoothly curved angles and clean, straight lines. This simplicity is also seen in their upholstery which is typically plain, with few patterns and rarely more than a single color. The design aesthetic is equally minimalistic and will feature either wood or metal and occasionally fiberglass.

When it comes to determining décor and rug choices, choosing patterns that fit the time period is crucial for tying each room together. This type of design includes lots of abstract patterns that were typically asymmetrical. Elements to avoid include anything that looks rustic which means no aged metal or unfinished wood in most cases. As far as lighting goes, lamps in this style are known to be either extremely straight, or extremely rounded. When it comes to adding extra elements of style, vintage art pieces can still be found with relative ease either at garage sales or at the local thrift store. With the right eye you can easily find the perfect accent pieces without breaking the bank.

The abundance of contrasting shapes means that you will have plenty of options for lighting every room. These lamps are mainly going to be made out of metal that has been finished, though wooden legs are not uncommon. Ceiling lamps are often made from exposed bulbs and straight metal rods, though numerous other designs are also fairly common. When creating this type of style your goal should be to let the wooden details take a majority of the focus which means going with wall color that is neutral and fabrics that have a softer hue.

Unlike the new Victorian style, midcentury modern is all about a less is more mentality which can be seen in the design of the furnishings and should be reflected throughout the space that you are redesigning. This minimalist look is naturally suited to smaller spaces that don't have the room, or the inclination, to seek out massive, heavy Victorian area pieces.

In order to achieve this, you will need to consider buying items with a high gloss finish, and use reflective surfaces to enhance the new crisp modern look. One of my personal favorite items to demonstrate this in a bedroom is a highly reflective mirrored bedside table. The bedside table is actually a mirror and it is fantastic because you see all of your room in the reflection and it enhances the look of your bed especially.

Beach stone: The beach stone style takes the traditional costal style in a more high end direction. The traditional costal style works most effectively when it calls to mind a hint of the beach without going completely overboard with and ensuring everything has shells or fish somewhere in the periphery. While the traditional style favors lots of bleached woods, the beach stone style, predictably, goes in a light stone or tile direction instead, including things like slate interior walls, title fireplaces or marble counter and bench tops.

Regardless of what colors you choose to go with, this style benefits heavily from two natural features of any home. The first of these features is abundant natural lighting as you are going to want your beach stone property to feel light and breezy, not cramped and dim. This naturally means that white is one of the colors most commonly used in this type of style as it amplifies light and spreads it across the room rather than soaking it all in. Light should definitely be the name of the game with this type of style as beach stone properties are going to typically feature plenty of skylights, big windows and glass doors to give the illusion that the indoors and the outdoors are blending together.

If you are interested in this style but don't have the natural lighting to pull it off, you can add a similar effect with lots of scones and lamps. Several carefully placed stone or tile accents can also help to move the light around the room. Mirrors with stone frames or a nice marble table top in the breakfast nook, polished to a shine, can help to artfully move the light around the room. When applying this effect, however, you will want to avoid adding so many glossy surfaces that it makes the room look hard.

Aside from white, colors are typically going to remain basic with this style, including lots of washed out colors and stripes that are tailored are also common. Layered on top of this you will want to consider pale neutrals to keep rooms from feeling either one dimensional or extremely austere. Common choices in these instances include khaki, beige or crème to evoke the general seaside theme without making it painfully obvious what it is you are going for. Additionally, an extremely light blue is another common bean stone color, both for stone or tile color or as an accent throughout the space and is especially common in bathrooms. Furthermore, finishes that are honed and matter will provide the colors with a chalky, almost soft bent that will contrast more starkly with the stone elements that you do chose to ad in.

Chapter 3: Main Living Room

New Victorian: If you have decided that you want to redo your living room in a new Victorian style then the first thing you are going to want to do is determine what you are going to keep modern and what you are going to want to do in a Victorian style. Remember, the key to this style is not leaning too hard in one direction or the other, which means planning out every step of the way to ensure you don't find yourself out of options when you are just about finished. The primary indicator of this style is the furniture, however, so odds are you are going to look into the types of classical furniture that you typically see associated with this design and then work backwards from there for the best results.

Depending on the amount of space you have available the type of furniture you will want to consider typically includes at least a chair, a couch and some type of table. This type of furniture can often become extremely pricey, extremely quickly, which means that if you are looking to save money a good place to start is online, you might consider a type of furniture that needs to be reupholstered. This furniture can then be redone in a more modern fabric choice, tying the room together and giving you a unique and one of a kind focal point in the process.

The classic Victorian color scheme is a contrast of bright shades and darker richer colors, and playing on this dichotomy can go a long way towards giving a room the classic, yet contemporary feel that you are looking for. Blues, yellows, violets, burgundies and shades of red are all very common to the time period and playing off this fact while using colors that would not have been around at the time is a great way to stay on theme while still opening yourself up to a wider (and brighter) range of color options. When painting a room, you could look at creating feature walls or having a boarder of white around the edge or your colored walls. To implement this, you would paint a white solid line around the perimeter of each wall in the room at about 30mm thick.

With this style, the wrong types of window treatments can spoil the entire look which is why it is important to generally forgo modern options and stick with classic tiebacks, valances or swags instead; ideally made from either damask, brocade or silk and trimmed with crystals, braids, cords or tassels. Like the furniture, these types of window treatments are key to the overall look which means that unless you come up with something truly spectacular, you should content yourself with coming up with alternative areas to add in a dash of modernity. If you are looking for a truly unique focal point for the room, consider a stained-glass window for a space saving, and era appropriate, option that is sure to be truly unique.

To give a room a Victorian feel without beating visitors over the head with the fact, a great option is to add in decorative archways, as well as other plasterwork ornamentation or moldings. This is a great way to add to the motif that you are going for without having to resort to cluttering up a room in the way that would make it truly Victorian. Alternatively, vintage wallpapers including ornate prints or metallic styling are a good choice, as are walls painted in rich, deep colors such as red or blue. When it comes to flooring, heavily pattern rugs or tile were the order of the day and can easily balance out the overall look if you choose a more modern room color instead.

Midcentury Modern: When it comes to making your living room not just look as though you bought some vintage furniture, but really give off the midcentury modern vibe, the first thing you are going to need to do is focus on getting rid of everything that is unnecessary. Midcentury modern was the beginning of the minimalism aesthetic that we are more familiar with today which means in order to pull it off successfully you are going to need to get rid of any of the clutter that is in the room. Furniture for this type of style is going to have clean lines, smooth curves and sculptural forms. The focal pieces for this room are all likely to be vintage pieces, large hanging lamps, wall art or even table and chairs from the era are often unique enough to draw the focus of the room all on their own.

Due to this less is more mentality, when it comes to choosing the pieces you are going to add into a room, only a few pieces will actually be needed to change the feel of the entire room. Things like a Noguchi coffee table or an Earnes lounger are iconic for a reason and their presence is enough to make the room read as midcentury modern in a big way. Other good living room options are side tables in an iconic midcentury design because they can fit into any room, and you can't go wrong with the other midcentury classic, the living room bar.

When it comes to the look of the room itself, the midcentury modern style has several options to choose from. First and foremost, the period is known for its fondness for geometric shapes and bold patterns, complete with intricate, sometime called psychedelic, designs. You can bring this style to mind through the use of bold rugs or drapes, or you can go all in and choose a wallpaper that represents this type of design aesthetic. When looking into these types of designs it is important to always keep in mind that these types of patterns should never overpower the general clean look that the space should be striving for. Don't forget that a little pattern goes a long way and if you overdo it you can lose the clean look you were going for and instead end up with a space that appears to be both cramped and cluttered no matter how big it actually is. When it comes to ensuring you have the right mix of patterns and neutral space, you should always skew in favor of neutral space.

When it comes to choosing a color palette that fits with the midcentury modern living room look, a neutral but warm color palette is often going to be the best choice. You are also going to want to embrace the natural differences in texture rather than painting the entire room the same way. This means that you are going to want to take your home's unique qualities into account during this process, midcentury modern has a streak of uniqueness to it that celebrates the characteristics that make each home different and celebrating those differences falls into the midcentury modern style even if the unique features don't in the broader sense of the term.

Beach Stone: The beach stone look is primarily focused on bringing the outdoors indoors which means you are going to want to start your interior design makeover by deciding where you will want to consider bringing distressed wood into the equation and where you want to use stone or tile instead. Whatever types of natural accents you decide to use, you are going to want to likely pick colors that will warm up the whites and blues that a traditional beach style is likely to use at one point or another. The goal of this type of space is for it to feel airy but still grounded, which is where the right types of stone accents can really come in handy. Stone accents in the form of picture frames and accessories balance out the wooden elements, which in turn balance out the crisp white that is often associated with this style.

While a traditional costal style may lean frequently on the nautical theme, especially when it comes to the wildlife, the beach stone style is a little more subdued in this way which means you will want to look for art and decorations that evoke the traditional feel without going so far as to beat your visitors over the head with the theme. The extra stone or tile in the room changes the feel of the traditional costal space somewhat and a cluttered space that is full of ocean life is likely going to feel counter to that ideal.

While the beach stone color pallet is full of different colors, they can all be traced back to three different inspirations, the sand, the sky and the waves. This means you are going to want to focus on seas blues which means watery aqua tones, navy and light grays which mimic the sea during a storm. You will also see a lot of muted greens, think sea glass, kelp and beach grass, as well as neutral colors like warm sand or the gray of driftwood. Finally, you will see lots of crisp white the color of canvas. There are not a lot of over -the-top patterns in this style, though stripes will certainly be seen from time to time.

When it comes to smaller accents, you will find that a little bit of sea glass and sand here or there will go a long way towards creating the overall feel that you are looking for in a subtle way that allows the room to be about more than just the fact that it has a nautical theme. A lamp with an open top can be filled with a small amount of sand and sea glass, or you can fill a vase partially with sea glass and the stick in a few small sticks of driftwood. White candles placed in a holder on top of sand and sea glass is a natural accent to practically any beach stone living room.

Chapter 4: Kitchen

New Victorian: When it comes to creating a kitchen in a modern Victorian style, the most natural choice is to start with a Victorian base, offset by the stark stainless steel efficiency of the modern kitchen. For example, Victorian kitchens were generally open and featured either L or U-based designs with an island in the center. To create a new Victorian look then, you can either create a classical looking kitchen surround a modern island or have a classical looking island accented by modern cabinets and drawers. Sinks are typically going to be of the farm style, surrounded by cabinets that are either wooden or stone.

The furniture that you choose for the space should be the opposite in theme to the island that you choose. This means modern if you choose a classical island or antique furniture if you go with a modern island. If you decide to go with a classical island design then you will want to consider repurposing cabinets, dressers, wardrobes and the like and taking advantage of their intricate carvings, unique hardware and classical moldings. On the other hand, if you decide to go with a modern island then you will want to consider something that is small and sleek to contrast the general size and weight that comes with the classic Victorian style. Materials besides wood and bright colors are also great ways to add in a bit of extra contrast without making it appear as though you are trying too hard.

Cabinets are a great way to add a slight Victorian flair to the room with things like crown moldings or overly elaborate hardware keeping the theme alive. Cabinets old or new could feature glass doors and shelves that are painting a bright color are a great way to make an otherwise darker room really pop. Traditional cabinets tend to trend towards lighter colors which means that dark countertops, even black, can add extra contrast to the room. A dark flooring in this room will also often create some need contrast when it comes to many traditional kitchen color schemes.

Accent colors in lighter colors of rose pink, purple, yellow and blue speak to the slightly romantic feel of many Victorian kitchens, a feeling that can be brought out in your own kitchen through the use of the right types of artwork. Common options are of traditional still-life paintings including common kitchen items like cheeses, wines, fruits and more which means that turning these assumptions on their heads is a great way to add a modern touch to a kitchen that is skewing too far towards the Victorian. Kitchen patterns often included flowery or otherwise floral designs and including a large hanging flowerbox in a kitchen window is another great way to add a dash of Victorian style to the proceedings.

Midcentury Modern: When it comes to designing a kitchen that has a sense of midcentury modern style, the biggest limiting factor is going to be your sense of scope. While you can go the traditional color scheme and new furniture, countertops, cabinets and floors route, you can also take thins a step further and purchase practically a complete suite of modern kitchen accessories in retro colors and styles. While these extras are fun to consider, they shouldn't be thought about until the specifics for the kitchen have been decided because there are so many different ways the redesign could go.

First and foremost, original midcentury kitchens were often fairly small, with a pair of countertops running parallel on either side. This type of design can be easily mimicked using a color scheme that is indicative of the era while at the same time taking advantage of modern material advances such as quartz countertops to extend the feeling of clean lines throughout the kitchen space as well.

If you are planning on doing a larger remodel, then another midcentury modern kitchen choice is to instead place the kitchen essentially in the center of its own room. Known as floating the kitchen, this design may seem counterintuitive at first but that is only because modern homes have settled into a uniform arrangement which places the kitchen sink against the way. The reality of the matter is that this type of kitchen can add to the general feeling of openness as well as minimalism that the midcentury modern look is going for. In this design the kitchen cabinets hang from the ceiling above a horseshoe of cabinets with the sink in the middle. This option is an especially good choice if your home has a small kitchen that is next to a larger dining room as it lets the former take advantage of the latter while also taking nothing away at the same time.

The midcentury modern style was the first style to start taking steps to creating an interplay between the indoors and the outdoors. If you are doing a complete remodel of the kitchen you can tap into this heritage by adding in large windows that reach from the ceiling to the bottoms of the countertops or all the way to the floor, connecting the interior and the exterior in the process. If you are looking to draw more light into the kitchen through the windows, then white countertops and cabinets are a good choice.

Beach Stone: When it comes to creating a beach stone look in the kitchen, the first thing that is going to have to go is any countertops that are not already granite. Granite countertops and a tile floor done in an appropriate color, contrasted with cabinets and high backed chairs made from reclaimed wood makes quite a first impression. If you are looking for more of a laid-back feel, consider choosing soft blue hues that you feel invoke the ocean breezes. This goes for your appliances as well as a surprising number can be found in one or more shades of aqua which will fit nicely into a wide variety of beach stone color schemes.

Additionally, while it might not call to mind a beach stone stile initially, you will be surprised what covering the plain drywall in the area around your kitchen with groove and tongue or shiplap paneling in either a vertical or horizontal position. This is a great way to add in some much-needed character to an otherwise drab space. You can even add the same to the ceiling and fronts of the existing cabinets before painting them for a more unified and stylized look. Another great touch is iridescent tile which can be added to backsplash areas for a look that is right on target that is right for practically any space regardless of how big or how small. The beauty of iridescent tile is that it is great for large areas that are otherwise boring yet unsuited for other types of options, but it can also be extremely effective when done in small amounts to add a splash of color to rooms that are done in darker neutral tones. If you don't want to use tile in the kitchen, a great option that is also in theme is to instead paint the floors using a high impact marine paint which is what is used to paint boat decks. Not only will this option hold up to anything you can through at it, it will evoke the precise theme you are looking to cultivate as well.

When it comes to lighting in your beach stone kitchen, a great choice is using what are known as textured pendant lights. These lights use textiles made from natural fibers to bring an earthy feel to the kitchen. For the right type of ambiance, you are going to want to always choose pendant lights that filter light in such a way that it diffuses from the bottom. Otherwise you are going to want your kitchen to be as open to natural light as possible which might mean adding in an extra window or two. The goal of any beach stone house is to be at one with the ideal elements outside the door and lots of natural light is the best way to show this feeling off.

Chapter 5: Bedrooms

New Victorian: A classic Victorian bedroom was known to contain plenty of one color flowered fabrics, heavy wallpaper and tables that were mostly covered. While including all three of these elements in your bedrooms might be considered overkill, choosing two to focus on while incorporating a more modern version of the third is a good way to keep the sort of balance that you are looking for with this particular style. In order to create the type of mostly classical look that you are striving for, some good places to start are with a new/old bedspread as well as traditional window coverings and rugs in the oriental, dhurrie or Axminister varieties. A quick and easy way to add a lot of Victorian flavor to any bedroom is via a wall canopy which can be installed easily just about anywhere.

If you are planning to use a flowered wallpaper in your bedrooms, a surefire choice for a classic Victorian feel that still provides you with lots of options when it comes to modernization, it is important that you take the time to carefully measure and draw out the floorplan before you start adding in the wallpaper as your goal should be to line up these patterns as meticulously as possible for the ultimate end results. Patterned or striped wallpaper is most common, though smaller flower patterns are also used.

Victorian bedrooms often favored softer colors that appear almost faded by the sun. Common primary colors for bedrooms include forest greens, subdued yellows, faded blues, violet purples and reds in the hue of a dusty rose. Furniture often includes overstuffed ottomans and chairs in floral patterns. When it comes to the window coverings, draperies are often a solid color in the soft hues outlined above, though they can also have a mild brocade or striping, but not if you have chosen a striped wallpaper. When it comes to creating extra privacy, you may want to include sheer panels that are made from net or white and cream lace which should include tiebacks of silk or velvet panels.

When using a wall canopy, it is important to match the bedspread to the fabric that is used if the same fabric cannot be used for both. Tables in the room could be covered in floor-length tablecloths of complimentary colors, though an easy way to create a focal point, and some modern contrast, is to go with a pair of modern bedside tables instead. The traditional Victorian bed is very large and massive, covered in either brass or polished wood, this is another option to go against the grain, however, and a modern bed amidst Victorian luxury can be an effective combination as well.

Midcentury Modern: The midcentury color palette is varied enough to ensure that no matter what type of room design you dream up there are plenty of color options to choose from. Abstract art is also always going to be on theme, the more colorful and abstract the better. Depending on the amount of space you have available, there are also plenty of on-theme storage options, with plenty of oddly shaped furniture and storage pieces taking up in thrift stores across the country just waiting for someone with the right 2 feet of extra space to come along.

Midcentury modern bedframes are typically low to the ground and sleek overall, often consisting of little more than the mattress and a frame on the ground seen from afar as to have no legs. These types of bedframes are readily available online and are an ideal choice when you are looking to make the most of a limited space, especially if you find one that includes storage underneath. The simple and clean line aesthetic applies as much in the bedroom as anywhere, which can take dedication, especially in smaller rooms where clutter is more naturally likely to accumulate.

One of the biggest keys to pulling of this type of look successfully is curating the right array of collectibles and art in your personal space. There are plenty of different period objects to choose from, just find the one that best represents you and go relatively crazy. This type of decorating is great because you should be able to easily deck out your space regardless of your budget as you can find either thrift store and reproduction items on the low end or original period art pieces on the high end with enough space in between for anyone at any interest level.

Midcentury modern allows you to go for the romantic bright reds of a rose. In your room to enhance the romance you could have a 3-way color scheme including rose red, black and white. Start off with crisp large white tiles leading up to a black sleek bedframe with a red duck feathered quilt cover and white throw pillows/rugs to complement the red. As in your bed you would love to see a white or mirrored bedside table with one decorative piece on top (potentially a really nice vase with fake roses inside). You will also need to have a large romantic picture of you as a couple or a city above the bed in black and white. This will bring a sense of love or adventure to the room. But you cannot get out of bed onto the tiles it would be too cold, so I strongly suggest a large soft plush red rug to comfort and warm your feet. Then continue along with the theme around the room with other pieces of furniture depending on the amount of space you have.

When it comes to choosing the right lighting for your bedroom, by going with the midcentury modern look you know that you have some of the most iconic light fixtures of the century in your repertoire. It doesn't matter if you are thinking about floor lamps or ceilings lamps, even original Noguchi light sculptures, you should be able to find either a reproduction, a vintage original or a modern take on the old style with relative ease. Rugs are bold with colors to contrast the more neutral tones of the walls, they are an easy way to spice up old floors, and practically any type of flooring is acceptable as long as it fits the color scheme that you have established. The overall goal should be a few points of bright color of interest in a primarily neutral background.

Beach Stone: The goal for any beach stone bedroom should be for it to feel as calm and restful as possible. This means you are going to want to focus first and foremost on choosing the right ocean color base to compliment this feeling. It doesn't matter what colors are typically thought of as soothing, it is important to be true to yourself and pick the colors that make you feel the most at ease. There is no right choice when it comes to the style of bed you want to look for to be in sync with the beach stone style, though if you have furniture in your bedroom that is darker, you might want to use a lighter color for the walls as a way of adding warmth to the space.

When it comes to choosing appropriate linens, again it is important to be inspired by the beach with only one or two colors, but not overly committed to it. When it comes to choosing the types of sheets that are right for the style, high thread count cotton sheets will have the crisp look that the style thrives on while still remaining extremely soft. A light, luxurious comforter should finish things off adding a sense of class as well as comfort to the proceedings.

When it comes to adding in an accent of stone or tile to the room, a fully tiled floor not only gives the room an extra sense of luxury but allows you to play with a wide variety of color combinations that might come across as over the top if carpeting is involved. While a traditional costal style would recommend wood floors, tile keeps the natural feel while taking the rest of the room from casual to classy. Other options include adding in a stone mantle to one of the walls or framing the focal point nautical painting that ties the room together in a stone frame.

When it comes to accessorizing, your goal should only be to directly reference the beach one time in your bedroom. Items that may be found on the beach but are also used in other contexts are acceptable, and even a great theme to try if you are looking for a challenge. Other great options things like terrariums, which you can fill with sand and sea glass as well as a bit of plant life as well to help the outdoors and indoors blend together properly. Lots of light, pale colors will help to open up the space and make those who walk in feel as though they are taking a breath of fresh air. To ensure that open feeling is in as full of effect as possible, you are going to want to remain very conscious of how much stuff you are packing into the space, remember, if the space stops feeling decorated and starts feeling cluttered then you have destroyed the central idea at the heart of this style.

Chapter 6: Bathrooms

New Victorian: When it comes to creating a bathroom that feels new Victorian, the best place to start is with the tile that is used. With the influx of online tile dealers, the patterns, shapes and colors that are readily available will cause your jaw to hit the floor. Practically, what this means is that the tile that you use for your flooring, and possibly as an accent elsewhere in the room, can easily represent a classic Victorian style on top of a modern twenty-first century color scheme. As with other patterns, Victorian bathroom tile patterns tend to lean in a flowery, flowing direction.

Victorian homes were all about creating a space that felt pampered and the bathroom is no different, this means you will want to think crown moldings, carved tables, lots of silver and gold and at least one tufted chair, stool or bench. Hardware is typically going to be gilt-metal or brass in style and will often feature elements that have been sculpted into things like scrollwork or flowers. Authentic hardware like this is widely available at estate and garage sale and will add a touch of realism to your room. Another classic Victorian piece is a large chest of drawers which is an easy way to add a Victorian feel to a bathroom that doesn't have room for lots of pomp and circumstance.

A sink basin as well as a bathtub done up in a Victorian style can be found easily online, while ornamentation for more modern accessories can help them play the part as well. The look you are going for with these items is freestanding, possibly claw footed, and with polished brass finishing if possible. There are numerous modern takes on the claw footed tub as well, playing into the classic and modern ideas at work with the new Victorian style all at once. Victorian shower doors typically opened from the center with a pair of handles in the middle, and recreating this look is an easy way to get your bathroom moving in the right direction. Likewise, an antique medicine cabinet can be tracked down at practically any estate sale and will add a dash of authenticity to the room.

Modern touches in this room typically come from accents and will include things like the rugs, towels, lighting and maybe some artwork. When working with your bathrooms, it is important to keep in mind that form should never supersede function in this space, especially when it comes to surfaces that are exceedingly slick. Depending on your space and your heating needs, adding in a modern freestanding radiator is a great way to ensure the room stays warm in the winter while also adding a modern piece that feels timeless in the process. When it comes to choosing linens for the room it is important to go as thick as possible, including the shower curtain.

Midcentury Modern: First things first, if you are going for a truly midcentury modern bathroom look, the first thing you are going to want to consider is a sink that features a more unique style than the basin that you might otherwise expect. Geometric shapes continue to be important, even in the bathroom, and a unique basin is a great focal point that sets the tone for the entire space. This style can easily be reflected in the tile either on the floor or on the walls where it only takes minor repeating patterns, done in a smaller tile, to create an overall effect that is in line with the target time period.

The bathroom is naturally a good place to call out some of the color the midcentury modern style is known for while also highlighting the style's love of different textures through the use of wooden cabinets and a marble countertop. As the goal should be minimalism, the cabinets should appear compact, with the basin sitting suspended above the cabinets. Rather than a medicine cabinet, use the space for a large round mirror to play up the geometric angle, perhaps emphasizing the choice with a unique hanging lamp that contains similar stylings. When it comes to looking into uniquely shaped lighting elements, it is important to take into account how much light they actually put off, especially in rooms like the bathroom where having the proper amount of light is rather important.

When it comes to choosing a color scheme, the midcentury modern style typically leans towards bathrooms that have darker ceilings while sticking with lighter walls. Timber flooring can be used, or more elaborate designs depending on the level of intensity of your remodel. If you are dealing with a smaller space, you will be happy to know that keeping storage space in the bathroom was a common trait among the first wave of midcentury modern spaces which means a second set of wooden cabinets for storage would not appear at all out of place.

The size of the space, even in a relatively large bathroom, means that it will be extremely easy for the space to appear as though it is cluttered. This means that you are going to need to be extremely careful when it comes to choosing art and accessories for the bathroom if you want to achieve the sense of lines and angles the minimalist feel the rest of the space should ideally be striving to capture.

When it comes to the shower space, freestanding tubs or showers that are enclosed in glass are the order of the day, with the starker the space surrounding the tub and the showerhead the better. This means no shower curtain if you can manage it, or one that is as simple and unobtrusive as possible otherwise, always pulled to one side and never creating an artificial barrier in the space.

Beach Stone: When it comes to creating a beach stone look in your bathroom, you are going to need to do more than simply replace the existing tile. To really show your commitment to the style, a great choice is a slate accent wall, preferably with a bluish grey hue. This can then easily be contrasted with some accent curtains in a stark white. If you are feeling repressed when it comes to the overall number of nautical pictures and paraphernalia, then the bathroom is the most appropriate place to get it out as the bathroom and the ocean have always been a natural style fit.

Alternatively, you can take the tile in the room to the next level and have the entire room done in the same color and style. As the color blue is often going to be the natural choice for many rooms due to its versatility, the bathroom can instead be a great place to explore the sandy part of the beach stone color spectrum. Various shades of sandy brown can make quite an impression when strewn across the entire room including the lighting and the fixtures. If you are going for a more modern look then an enclosed glass shower will keep the theme alive while a clawfoot tub and crisp white shower curtain tied back with a relevant accent color may be a better fit instead.

When it comes to the sink, a marble countertop not only adds a splash of elegance to the room, but it remains completely on style as well. What's more, when you go shopping for the countertop for your bathroom, you can confidently know that you are going to get the best piece of marble at the best price around. The fact of the matter is that because you are going to be cutting a rather large hole out of it anyway, you are going to be able to choose the cream of the crop that just happens to have a major flaw in one area. Cut out the flaw and reap the rewards.

Chapter 7: Backyard

Alongside interior design is the backyard; it is important to maintain the theme/ style of your home. Carryout the same design principles in doing your back yard, it is not always simply creating a nice back yard and patio. It is more than that the key to an overall nice home is being able to tie everything in together and create harmony and compatibility.

New Victorian: At the heart of the classic Victorian backyard was the lawn.   The well-kept, manicured and spacious green lawn was a centerpiece of the outdoor area. Tea parties and evening gatherings were often held within this space. The lawn area was expansive, and always expertly maintained. In modern times, while we still often hold outdoor parties and barbeques on hot summer days, the grassy central area to hold the majority of the gathering has been replaced with the more convenient concrete patio or stone-covered pavement. A blend between these two preferences would nicely accommodate both modern and Victorian ideals. Consider having a paved sidewalk lead to the central table area encapsulated within the yard. While the dining or entertaining area would still contain stoned pavement or concrete, it would be surrounded by an expansive and uniformly luscious green lawn. This would allow guests to keep their feet from interacting with the grass if that was their wish, but they could still benefit from the aesthetics that the lawn has to offer.

After you've figured out how you want to set the balance between the concrete and the lawn, the next part of the lawn design equation that you should consider is the garden. Similar to their grass, the Victorians were known for adorning their backyards with flowerbeds that were both uniform and consistent with the color schemes of their time. Blue, yellow and violet flowerbeds were frequently seen on the outside of the Victorian home. If you were to follow the New Victorian tradition, you could arrange flower beds on the outer edges of the patio area, but consider planting the flowers in a mismatched pattern. Instead of keeping all of the blues, yellows and purples separate from one another, you could mismatch them. This way, the color scheme remains consistent with the Victorian era, but with a slightly more colorful and modern twist.

As for the furniture, it seems as though some of the old Victorian traditions are modern once more, so it shouldn't be too difficult to find furniture that will fully adhere to the look that you're trying to create. As was already discussed in previous chapters, the tables and chairs that were prevalent in the Victorian era consisted of elaborate carving and drastic ornamentation. Their outdoor furniture was no different.

If you're looking to keep the Victorian influence on your backward to a tasteful amount, a good option would be to purchase a modern patio table that has the ability to hold an umbrella. The table would bear little carvings, would be made of iron, and have a relatively simple design. The possibility for an umbrella would allow you to decorate this space with a flowered pattern overhead, or some other type of pattern that fits the Victorian style. Again, while you want the Victorian elements of the design to speak the space, you also want to avoid going overboard. Other types of furnishings that you can give to this space include a chimenea and rocking chairs.

Midcentury Modern: The foundation of the midcentury modern backyard is either wood or concrete. If you are fond of this style, the backyard is no exception to these rules. Merbau Wooden decks and concrete slabs that are separated by only a few inches to reveal small amount of grass work well for the minimalistic feel that the midcentury modern décor promotes. The primary areas of this type of backyard space will contain little grass, and should have neutral colored-plants on the outskirts of the central patio area. While asymmetry and contrasting shapes can be considered central to the midcentury modern theme, these ideals should be found through the furnishings of the deck area, rather than through the foundation of the space. It's a good idea to keep the base of this space neat and simple, rather than go for anything outlandish or obnoxious. This will set the tone for the backyard as a whole.

As was just mentioned, a successful midcentury modern backyard will contain little grass. Instead, it will be adorned with simple plants that are neutral in color. A few types of plants that are both simple in design and hue include:

- **The Yucca Plant:** You have probably seen a Yucca plant before but you may not have realized it. These plants can be characterized by their pointy, green and sword-like appendages. This plant will provide your garden with a southwestern feel, and are mostly planted in drought-prone areas. They also come in more than one color which helps us with our color schemes.
- **The Carex Plant:** It's likely that you've seen this plant before as well. It's the plant that you've looked at and thought, "this looks soft", but upon touching it found it to be rough and a tad prickly in your hand. The Carex plant is tan to beige in color, and is mostly revered for its wispy and strong-looking qualities. Its wispiness is able to bring more movement to your garden, while still keeping with the midcentury modern color tones that were discussed in earlier chapters of this book.

The furniture found in midcentury modern backyards are mostly made of wood or metal. As of writing this in the year 2016, it seems as though wood as securely become more popular than metal in terms of decorative use. This being the case, it would be a good idea to approach the furnishings of your backyard with wood in mind. Slatted wood to be used for the table is always a good option for this type of design. If wood simply isn't your preference for the outdoor area, consider instead the dull color tones of the rest of the area. Rather than using a chimenea to warm the bodies of your guests as was suggested for the New Victorian era style, a stone fire pit would be a better option. Lastly, the string lights that are currently popular would go great in a midcentury modern space, as long as the lights themselves have an industrial feel to them. Consider lights that have a chrome string attached to them, or ones that comprise halogen bulbs.

Beach Stone: The beach stone style exists based on the notion that the ambiance of the space should feel breezy and relaxing like the beach, but without any of the disturbances that the beach can bring with it. This being the case, your best bet when furnishing your patio in the beach stone style is to stay away from the desire to put sand in your backyard. Of course, it might seem like you would want to pay homage to the beach in this way, but sand can get in your shoes. If you're not wearing sandals of if it rains, sand will be uncomfortable to walk in. While some people do indeed put sand in their backyard and consider it "beach stone", the classier look is to instead adorn this area of your home with plenty of stones. A large stone walkway with smaller stones embedded into the periphery of the walkway is aesthetically pleasing to this style. While grass is not crucial to the overall look of this type of backyard, it's also not sacrilege. If you have grass in your backyard, the beach stone style can still work for you, as long as you are creative with your stone placement throughout the yard.

The beach stone style is definitely enhanced by water. While everyone may not have the means to install a pool or a pond into their backyard, any body of water is better than none for this aesthetic. For example, if you live in a place where water is nearby, you could install an outdoor spritzer, so that your loved ones and guests could wash off after being at the beach or by the pool. If access to water isn't a problem for you and you already own a pool, consider having it redone to include a water slide and paved in stone. If you want to get even fancier, you can have the waterslide feature a waterfall, with water moving down the wall of the slide and into the pool. This will provide the centerpiece of your yard with more movement, and will complement the oceanic theme of the entire space. Additionally, let's not forget that chlorine water is typically blue or clear, which provides color that certainly complements the undertones of the beach stone theme.

The furnishings of a backyard that is looking to adopt the beach stone style should be neutral and easy. Unlike the tones that exist in the midcentury modern style or the vibrancy that is featured in the New Victorian style, these colors should remind you and your visitors of the beach, the water, and the sun. To accomplish this, consider Adirondack chairs that are white or khaki in color. Slatted wood also works for this look, but wider slabs are typically preferred to slimmer ones. This is due to the fact that wider slats serve as a reminder of the boardwalk for most people. Lastly, the emphasis on lighting that this style appreciates should not be a problem for this outdoor area. If you live in a sunny and well-weathered area, the beach stone design will likely be complemented by the natural light that already accentuates this space.

Conclusion

Thank you for downloading and reading this novella on Interior design. Let's hope it was informative and able to provide you with all of the tools you need to achieve your goals whatever it is that they may be. Just because you've finished this book doesn't mean there is nothing left to learn on the topic, expanding your horizons is the only way to find the mastery you seek.

The next step is to stop reading already and start deciding on what type of interior design refresh is not only right for your property, but a right match for your personality as well. When you are planning out your renovations, it is important to keep in mind that if you have to cut costs, what you are really doing is cutting quality. Unless you are an expert contractor, odds are you will not be able to provide the quality of results that someone who does the task for a living is going to do, no matter how much you save. Likewise, if you use cheap materials then you run the risk of them breaking sooner than later, leaving you in the position of wishing you had bought the higher quality product in the first place. Worse than this though is if the end result looks cheap, only because it is reflecting the quality of the products.

If you are having difficulty justifying the high costs throughout, it is important to keep in mind that you get what you pay for in these situations and you are going to be stuck looking at the results for a long time. Don't forget, a high quality interior design renovation can add significant value to your property, invest in the future and live your dream! Finally, if you enjoyed or found this book useful, please take the time to leave me a positive review on Amazon! I appreciate your feedback, and it really helps me to continue producing high quality books.

www.ingramcontent.com/pod-product-compliance
Lightning Source LLC
Chambersburg PA
CBHW050856290526
45792CB00002B/611